NAVY SEALs
Mission at the Caves

SPECIAL OPERATIONS FILES

NAVY SEALs
Mission at the Caves

Brandon Webb
with Thea Feldman

Henry Holt and Company

New York

This book is dedicated to the next generation who have the ability to reach far beyond imagination and capture their dreams in real life.
—B.W.

Henry Holt and Company, *Publishers since 1866*
Henry Holt® is a registered trademark of
Macmillan Publishing Group, LLC
175 Fifth Avenue, New York, NY 10010
mackids.com

Produced by Stonesong Press, LLC
Designed by Jessica Nordskog

Library of Congress Control Number: 2018936457

Our books may be purchased in bulk for promotional, educational,
or business use. Please contact your local bookseller or the Macmillan
Corporate and Premium Sales Department at (800) 221-7945 ext. 5442
or by e-mail at MacmillanSpecialMarkets@macmillan.com.

First edition, 2018
Printed in the United States of America by
LSC Communications, Harrisonburg, Virginia

ISBN 978-1-250-11468-6 (hardcover)
10 9 8 7 6 5 4 3 2 1

ISBN 978-1-250-19427-5 (paperback)
10 9 8 7 6 5 4 3 2 1

This is a fictionalized account of
an actual Navy SEALs mission.

THE AUTHOR, BRANDON WEBB, pictured in Niland, California, during training.

Introduction

Hi. I'm Brandon Webb. I served in the United States military as a Navy SEAL sniper. I was privileged to serve my country during a very important time in history.

You are about to read about my life as a SEAL. You will read all about a SEALs mission at dangerous caves in the mountains of Afghanistan.

The SEALs (Sea, Air, and Land) are the

Special Operations Force of the United States Navy. We are trained to conduct special missions. As you will read, being a Navy SEAL is actually all about training. And training some more. And some more after that. You train to become a Navy SEAL. Then, you keep training, so you will be ready when you're sent on a mission.

Each mission requires quick action (the *right* action) and quick thinking. Our goal? Hit the ground running and get it done before the enemy even knows we're there.

The US Army, Marines, and Air Force also each have their own Special Ops Forces, or Spec Ops. All Spec Ops guys are highly trained. They have to be.

A lot of Spec Ops missions are about fighting back against terrorism. What is terrorism? Basically, it is when a person or a group uses violence for political, religious, or other reasons.

In this series I will introduce you to one guy from each of the US military's Spec Ops Forces. You will read about their lives and about how they served their country.

I decided to tell my own story in the third person. That's because that's how I will tell you each of the other Spec Ops Forces stories.

I was proud to help defend my country. And I'm honored to share my story with you.

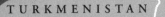

TURKMENISTAN

UZBEKISTAN

■ KABUL

AFGHANISTAN

ISLAMABAD ■

Punjab

PAKISTAN

KHOST

4

CHAPTER 1

January 6, 2002, early morning
Zhawar Kili Caves
Khost, Afghanistan

Brandon Webb and the other members of Navy SEAL Team 3 paused. They were outside the Zhawar Kili caves. It was not yet dawn.

In the middle of the night, they had boarded military helicopters. The helicopters landed in the mountains. Then, in the dark, the men walked 7.5 miles to the caves. The mountain air in Khost, Afghanistan, was cool before dawn. It was also filled with tension.

The caves had a long history. In 1989, Osama bin Laden had declared war on the United States from them. He was the founder of the terrorist group called al Qaeda. Now the Taliban, another

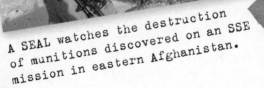

A SEAL watches the destruction of munitions discovered on an SSE mission in eastern Afghanistan.

terrorist group, was using the caves. The caves were one of the largest Taliban terrorist training camps in Afghanistan. They were well hidden and well protected in the mountains.

The US military wanted to shut down the training camp. The night before, the military pounded the area with Joint Direct Attack Munitions (JDAMs). Today, Brandon's platoon was going into the caves. They would look for any survivors. They would also collect information and equipment. Then they would radio air support with their exact location. More bombs would destroy whatever was left.

The entire mission was supposed to take twelve hours.

Brandon kept his breathing slow and

steady. He waited with the other men for the signal to go in. None of them knew what they would find. Would the caves be booby-trapped? Would there be armed terrorists waiting inside? No one knew. But they were trained Navy SEALs. They were ready for anything.

Twenty Marines were also there. They were fanned out on a ridge high above the caves. They would cover the SEALs down below. They would deal with anyone who tried to enter the caves while the SEALs were inside.

The signal came. The men went to work. They cleared the caves, one at a time. Four men moved quickly into a cave. They turned sharply around tight spaces and corners.

The JDAMs from the night before had done their job in the first caves. Brandon stepped over rubble. There was shattered equipment and furniture. There were also the remains of human bodies. A lot of them.

Some of the caves were very dark and deep. The men had night-vision goggles, but they didn't do much. The goggles needed a tiny bit of natural light to work. These caves were pitch-black. The SEALs used their flashlights. They used the small beams of light mounted on their weapons, too.

Brandon and the others could see that the bombs had not reached the deep caves. They found a medical clinic. There was also a kitchen and several sleeping areas. There was a mosque and more.

The SEALs did not find any people. They did find a lot of ammunition and fuel. It was stacked from floor to ceiling. It looked like this one US mission might have stopped many terrorist attacks.

Brandon entered a classroom. There were posters on the walls. The posters had anti-American words and pictures. He stopped in front of one poster. It had a photo of Osama bin Laden in the center. In the background, two airplanes crashed into the Twin Towers of the World Trade Center in Lower Manhattan.

"What the . . . ?" Brandon said. He realized the photo was doctored. This poster had been created way before the day of the actual attack. It was probably meant to "inspire" terrorists in training.

"This is hands down the creepiest thing in here," Brandon said to the other SEALs. It was also a strong reminder of why he was there in the first place.

A propaganda poster depicting Osama bin Laden, recovered from an al Qaeda classroom.

USS COLE

CHAPTER

2

October 12, 2000
Gulf of Aden, Yemen

More than a year before the mission at the caves, Brandon was on his first deployment as a Navy SEAL sniper. His platoon was on the USS *Duluth*. Their mission was to stop Iraqi tankers from smuggling oil out of Iraq. At the time, the US military was not involved in any major conflicts anywhere in the world.

That was about to change.

On October 12, 2000, the *Duluth* was in Bahrain. The men got word that another American ship had been attacked. The ship was the USS *Cole*. The damage was bad.

Al Qaeda suicide bombers piloted a 35-foot boat loaded with explosive into the USS *Cole*.

The *Cole* was not far away. It was in the nearby Gulf of Aden in Yemen. It had stopped there to refuel. Two men in a speedboat approached the ship. No one knew it at the time, but the speedboat was filled with explosives. The speedboat rammed into the *Cole*. The speedboat blew up. The two men on board were killed. Seventeen sailors on the *Cole* were killed. Thirty-nine more sailors were injured. The attack left a gaping 40-foot hole in the side of the ship.

The *Duluth* immediately headed to the scene. The Marines had already arrived. They had set up a defensive area around the *Cole*. The remaining crew members of the *Cole* were hard at work. They were trying to prevent the huge ship from sinking.

The SEALs set up a sniper team on the bridge of the *Cole*. The snipers would make sure no other terrorists got near the ship. Brandon was part of the sniper team. So was fellow Navy SEAL sniper Glen Doherty. They took turns on watch. They worked around the clock. Each shift was twelve hours long. Each man had a .50 caliber sniper rifle and four LAW rockets with him on the bridge.

The United States and Yemen did not

SNIPER RIFLE

have a great relationship. There was a lot of anti-American feeling in Yemen. Yemen also had a history of helping terrorists. During his shifts on the bridge, Brandon could sense Yemeni weapons were trained on the *Cole*. "This is one *serious* standoff," he said to Glen at a shift change.

A few boats got close to the *Cole*. None, though, crossed the invisible line the Marines and SEALs had set up around it. Eventually, the *Cole* was hauled back to the United States. It took fourteen months to repair.

Brandon realized that this attack was different from any other. A small speedboat had crippled a huge naval destroyer. Two men with homemade explosives had killed seventeen military men. They had injured thirty-nine more. The side that had seemed less powerful had won. This was a new kind of terrorism.

Osama bin Laden's al Qaeda claimed responsibility for the attack on the USS *Cole*. Their next attacks were already in the works.

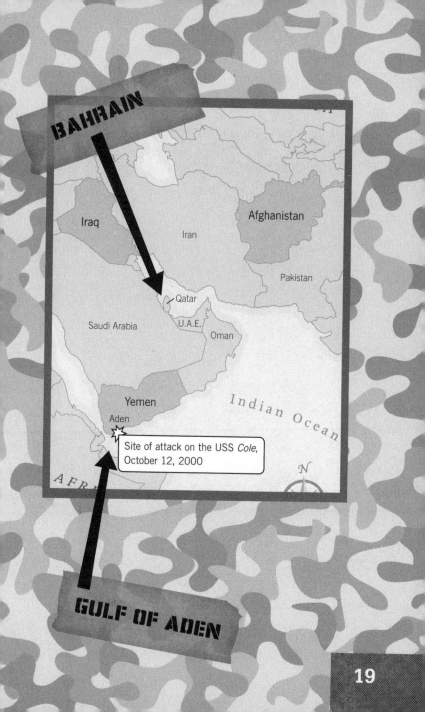

BAHRAIN

GULF OF ADEN

Iraq

Afghanistan

Iran

Pakistan

Qatar

Saudi Arabia

U.A.E.

Oman

Yemen

Indian Ocean

Aden

Site of attack on the USS *Cole*,
October 12, 2000

N

AFR

20

CHAPTER

3

September 11, 2001

That morning, there was barely a cloud in the sky. The sky was a brilliant shade of blue. Everyone hurrying to school or work or to the airport noticed how beautiful the day was. That is not what September 11, 2001, is remembered for.

At 8:46 A.M., terrorist hijackers crashed American Airlines Flight 11 into the North Tower of the World Trade Center in downtown New York City.

At 9:03 A.M., United Airlines Flight 175 crashed into the South Tower. Everyone on board both planes died. Thousands of people in the two buildings were also killed. Some died from the force of the crashes. Some died from the raging fires that the crashes started. Others died when the buildings collapsed.

A total of 2,606 people in the two buildings and surrounding area were killed.

At 9:37 A.M., American Airlines Flight 77 crashed into the Pentagon in Arlington, Virginia. The Pentagon is the headquarters of the US Department of

Defense. The Department of Defense is in charge of the US Armed Forces and all US

Smoke rises after two planes collided with the World Trade Center in a terrorist attack on September 11, 2001.

agencies that deal with national security. The force of the crash started a huge fire. Five stories in one section of the Pentagon collapsed. One hundred and twenty-five people died.

At 10:03 A.M., United Airlines Flight 93 crashed in a field near Shanksville, Pennsylvania. The passengers on board

A plane was hijacked and crashed into the side of the Pentagon just after two plane hit the World Trade Center on 9/11.

had heard about the other attacks. They fought the hijackers for control of the plane. They did not want this plane to hit anything. All forty-four people on board Flight 93 were killed upon impact.

A total of 265 people in the four airplanes were killed. This included nineteen hijackers. In all, on that day, 2,996 people were killed. More than 6,000 others were injured.

It was the first attack on the mainland United States by foreign enemies. The day became known as 9/11. No terrorist organization stepped forward to claim responsibility. Investigators worked quickly. They linked all the hijackers to al Qaeda and Osama bin Laden.

Brandon was stateside when the attacks happened. He was between deployments overseas. He was home in California with his wife, Gabriele.

At the crack of dawn that morning, Brandon was surfing. He enjoyed riding the strong waves. The morning air was cool and crisp. The only sounds were the ocean waves and the seagulls.

When Brandon got back to his house, Gabriele was in front of the television. "Brandon," she said. "We're under attack."

"What are you talking about?" asked Brandon. Then he looked at the TV. He saw the live broadcast of what was happening. "This is unbelievable!" said Brandon. He could not take his eyes off the screen.

Brandon was eager to get back over-seas. The 9/11 attacks made him want to defend his country more than ever. But this was something he had first dreamed of doing when he was just a teenager.

The Navy SEAL insignia (nicknamed "the Budweiser") is awarded to soldiers who pass the rigorous training to become a Navy SEAL.

BRANDON, AGE 13

CHAPTER

4

■**I**■n 1987, when Brandon was about thirteen years old, he got a summer job. He went to work on a dive boat called the *Peace*. A man named Bill Magee owned the boat. People rented the boat to go scuba diving.

The *Peace* was docked in the harbor in Ventura, California. Brandon and his family had their own boat. It was called the *Agio*. Brandon's family lived on the *Agio* at that time.

Brandon had always been very strong. He was a good athlete, too. He was able to do whatever was needed on the *Peace*. He was the most junior guy on the boat. So he had to do chores no one else wanted to do. This included diving down to free the boat's anchor if it got stuck on something. Sometimes this happened in the middle of the night. Brandon would be shaken out of a deep sleep. Within minutes, he would be in the dark water with a flashlight.

"So much for my fear of the dark," he said before taking the plunge one night. "Never mind my fear of sharks." Brandon was terrified at first. He soon got over his fears. He quickly grew to love these nighttime dives.

Brandon, age 16, aboard the *Peace*, where he first got his taste for diving.

Brandon loved everything about working on the *Peace*. He became an expert diver. He eventually became a rescue diver, too. He also became skilled at stalking and hunting fish in open water.

He had great relationships with Bill Magee and the boat's captain, Michael Roach. "These guys are all about respect and responsibility," said Brandon. "They have me thinking I can be somebody. Maybe I really can do something special with my life."

Brandon worked on the *Peace* every summer for the next few years. At the end of Brandon's freshman year in high school, his parents decided to sail around the world in the *Agio*.

"I really don't want to go," Brandon thought. "I've got more important things to do than sail around the world with my family. Like dive, surf, date, and get my driver's license."

He hoped his parents would change their minds, but they didn't. Brandon and his younger sister, Rhiannon, were put on independent studies for a year. Then the family set sail.

Even though he had not wanted to take the trip, Brandon enjoyed a lot of the time out at sea. He and his sister watched dolphins jump and play in the water near the *Agio*. They all caught a lot of fish, which they cooked and ate for dinner.

Everyone did chores on the boat. Brandon and his father split night watch.

During his shift, Brandon was the only one awake from midnight until 4:00 A.M. "Wow!" he said each night when he looked up at the stars in the sky for the first time. Out in the middle of open water you could see the stars much better than you could from land.

Within a month at sea, Brandon finished his schoolwork for the entire year. He also read a ton of books. He taught himself to juggle. And he practiced navigating the old-fashioned way: by using the stars. Long before electronic equipment was invented to help people sail from one place to another, people used the stars to guide them.

The family had sailed from San Diego, California, all the way to Papeete, Tahiti, in just thirty days. They had stopped at several places in Mexico and in the Marquesas Islands. Unfortunately, during the trip, Brandon and his father were having a lot of trouble getting along. They fought over how to manage the boat. Brandon had learned a lot on the *Peace*. He wanted a say on the *Agio*.

"Look," Brandon said in frustration. "I know what I'm doing."

His father replied, "There's only one captain on this boat. And you know who that is."

Brandon knew he was being a teenager with a bad attitude. He just couldn't help himself. He kept challenging his dad. The two kept fighting. Rhiannon stayed in her room to get away from the tension.

Brandon's mom tried to make peace. She would beg Brandon, "Please just chill out. I know you have a lot of experience, but this *is* your dad's boat."

The arguments continued. One day, Brandon's dad had had enough. He told his son, "You're off the boat. Get your stuff and find yourself passage aboard another boat. Go wherever you want. I'm done. I mean it."

Brandon was shocked. And scared. He was also relieved, because he knew he and his dad could not keep fighting this way. His mom pleaded and pleaded with Brandon's dad to change his mind. He would not. So Brandon's mom arranged for Brandon to go back to Bill Magee and the *Peace*. She even got him on another boat, *Shilo*, as a crew member. The *Shilo* was docked in Tahiti and headed for Hawaii.

Brandon was busy working on the *Shilo* during the day. At night he was alone with his thoughts. "My whole family is gone," he thought. "I am truly alone." The first few nights he cried himself to sleep. He knew his dad was right: there *is* only one captain on a boat. But he still felt his dad hadn't always made the right decisions. He did not regret speaking up for himself.

Once in Hawaii, Brandon flew back to California. There, he went back to work on the *Peace*. Because he had already done all his schoolwork for the year, he was able to work on the boat full-time.

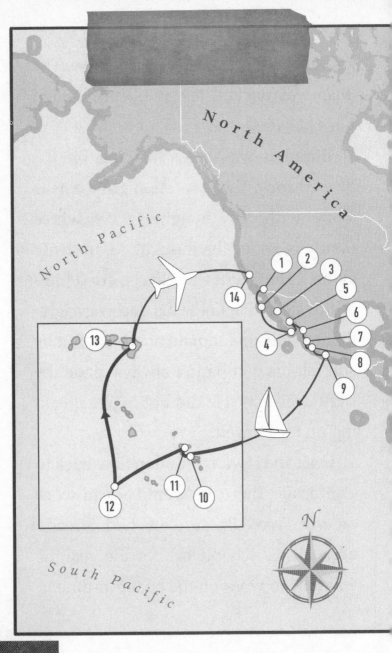

One day a group showed up for a few days of diving. Some of the guys really impressed Brandon. They were rugged and clearly knew what they were doing. But they did not show off in the least. They did not act tough or have any kind of attitude.

In turn, the guys were impressed with how serious a diver Brandon was. One of the guys started chatting with Brandon.

BRANDON'S FAMILY TRIP

1	San Diego, California	10	Hiva Oa, Marquesas Islands
2	Guadalupe Island, Mexico	11	Nuku Hiva, Marquesas Islands
3	Baja, Mexico	12	Papeete, Tahiti
4	Cabo San Lucas, Mexico		
5	La Paz, Mexico		**BRANDON ON HIS OWN**
6	Mazatlán, Mexico	13	Hilo, Hawaii
7	Puerto Vallarta, Mexico	14	Ventura, California
8	Manzanillo, Mexico		
9	Acapulco, Mexico		

"You know," the guy said, "you should check out the SEALs."

Brandon was confused. He had no idea why the guy was talking about seals. "Is this guy into seals the way some people are into whale watching?" he wondered. Or was the guy making some kind of joke? Brandon did not get it.

The guy saw the look on Brandon's face. "I mean SEALs," he explained. "As in the Navy maritime Special Operations Forces. SEAL stands for Sea, Air, and Land. SEALs. To become a SEAL," he added, "you go through the toughest military training in the world."

Brandon had never heard of them. He realized, though, that these guys *were* Navy SEALs. "That's what makes them stand out the way they do," he thought. He also liked what this guy was saying about becoming and being a SEAL.

Brandon thought for a minute. "I love the water," he reasoned. "And I'm a pretty good diver. This sounds like it could be the right challenge for me." Suddenly, he knew that it was. At age sixteen, Brandon had found his calling. "I'm going to become a Navy SEAL," he said.

CHAPTER

5

As soon as Brandon graduated from high school, he enlisted in the Navy. By now, he and his dad had made their peace. And his dad totally supported Brandon's decision.

Brandon arrived at boot camp in Orlando, Florida, with his fellow recruits at 10:00 at night. At 4:00 the next morning, senior recruits woke them up. They were yelling and banging on aluminum trash cans. This wake-up call set the tone for boot camp.

Brandon had always been physically active. He was in good shape. His time on the *Peace* had taught him many things that would help him in the Navy. He had learned how to be part of a team. He had learned how to respect authority, how to work hard, and much more. But one thing he had no experience with was how to walk in step with the ninety-nine other new recruits in his company!

The new recruits had to learn to walk in step together. They had to pivot, turn, march right, and march left together.

During training, every time anyone messed up, the entire company had to drop to the pavement. They had to do ten or more push-ups. Then they had to get up and keep practicing.

Before long, someone else messed up. So down they all went to the pavement again. This was one of the most

Recruits stand in formation in front of Recruit Training Command, the Navy's only boot camp facility.

unexpectedly grueling parts of the early training.

A few weeks into basic training, a SEAL recruiter arrived. He showed a video that described the life of a SEAL. Brandon

A sailor hangs from a Seahawk helicopter during an open-water search-and-rescue training.

watched guys being tested underwater, shivering in the cold, and going through BUD/S training. BUD/S stands for Basic Underwater Demolition/SEAL. It is the name of the Navy SEAL training program. In order to become a Navy SEAL, you first must get through basic Navy boot camp. After that, if you qualify, you can begin BUD/S. A lot of guys want to be Navy SEALs. Only a few are accepted into the training program. Of those, most will drop out or be disqualified. BUD/S is that tough.

Brandon and a few other men in his company were interested. They had to sign up for pre-BUD/S workouts. This meant they had to get up at 4:45 A.M. every day. That was an hour before the rest of their company.

Every morning they warmed up with one hundred push-ups. Then they did one thousand flutter kicks. A flutter kick is when you lie on your back with your hands under you and scissor-kick your legs in the air. Next were dozens and dozens of pull-ups. They did all this every day. *Before* regular boot camp training. Five guys signed up. Brandon and one other guy were the only two to keep going.

While Brandon trained, he waited for his orders to report to BUD/S. Then he found out that he wasn't going to go straight from boot camp to BUD/S.

"Sorry, Webb," one of the SEALs told him. "It turns out you have orders to Search and Rescue. They're under-

Two soldiers are recovered during
search-and-rescue training aboard
the USS *San Jacinto*.

manned, so we can't just yank you out
and put you in BUD/S. You'll have to
wait and apply for a transfer later on."

It turned out to be four years before Brandon got to BUD/S. But he learned an awful lot during that time. Before he even went to Search and Rescue (SAR), he went to Naval Air Crew Candidate School (NACCS). There, he learned to fly under all kinds of conditions.

SAR was next. This training involved a lot of swimming. He also spent a lot of time in an indoor pool. The pool made waves that were just like ocean waves. In this pool, Brandon learned how to save the lives of airmen whose aircraft had gone down in freezing-cold water. SAR was hard, but Brandon's years of experience working in the water helped him.

Brandon became a SAR graduate. But he still didn't go to BUD/S. Instead, he had to pick an "A" school. Everyone in the Navy goes through "A" school after boot camp. It's where graduates get special training for whatever specific job in the Navy they want to do. Brandon decided to learn how to operate the sonar equipment on a helicopter.

Brandon finished "A" school. He kept training. He also deployed as part of an active helicopter squadron. After that, he deployed twice on aircraft carriers in the western Pacific Ocean. When he got back from the second western Pacific deployment, his orders to BUD/S were waiting for him.

There had been many twists and turns along the way. But Brandon had never given up.

There was one more challenge. Before Brandon could start BUD/S, he had to pass a Physical Screening Test (PST). Here is an overview of the test:

- 500-yard (457-meter) swim: breaststroke or sidestroke

  Time requirement: 12.5 minutes or less (9 minutes or less is preferred)

- 42 or more push-ups in 2 minutes (at least 100 to be seen as competitive)

- 50 or more sit-ups in 2 minutes (again, 100 or more is the goal)

- 6 or more pull-ups from a dead hang

  Time requirement: none (12 or more is preferred)

- 1.5-mile (2.4-kilometer) run in boots and pants

  Time requirement: under 11.5 minutes (under 9 minutes is considered competitive)

Brandon took the test and—he failed! His run time was twelve minutes, a full thirty seconds over the slowest acceptable time. Brandon was completely shocked. After waiting so long to get to BUD/S, he had run into the most unexpected obstacle of all: himself.

"I am not going to feel sorry for myself," said Brandon. And he didn't. He practiced each part of that test over and over. Then he took it again. This time he passed. Brandon was on his way to BUD/S at last.

HOOYAH!

6

On June 14, 1997, Brandon checked in for BUD/S training. One of the first things he saw was a BUD/S class doing their workout outside on the Grinder. The Grinder is a black concrete-and-asphalt courtyard. It is famous as a place where recruits go through punishing workouts.

The men were doing push-ups. Brandon heard the instructor call out, "Fifty! Fifty-one!" He heard a few recruits call out "Hooyah!" in response. "Hooyah" is a special SEALs word. It can mean many things. It can mean "Yes, instructor!" Or it can mean an obscenity. In this instance, perhaps it meant both?

The bell is a fixture of Hell Week; trainees ma ring the bell, signaling that they quit if the; decide the training is too much for them.

Brandon noticed something else. He saw the famous brass bell. The bell had a worn rope hanging down from its ringer. The bell was just off the edge of the concrete. Right near the bell were more than one hundred helmets. Each helmet had a SEAL-in-training's name on it.

No SEAL in training wanted to go near that bell. No SEAL in training wanted his helmet to join those on the ground. If you rang that bell three times, it meant you could not go any further. It meant the training was too hard for you. You quit. You put your helmet down and you left.

Brandon was determined. He would never ring that bell. He would never quit.

Brandon was in Class 215, which started with 220 men. BUD/S training has three different phases or parts. Before the first phase, the men go through a five-week indoctrination period called indoc.

The first week of indoc included a repeat of the BUD/S PST. Twenty guys failed. Nearly ten percent of the class was out already. Brandon knew the odds of making it all the way through BUD/S were stacked against him.

First Phase is all about physical conditioning. When First Phase started, Brandon was worried that he wasn't physically fit enough to get through the tough exercises. Then a super-strong guy quit during the first week. This taught Brandon something very important. Getting through BUD/S, he realized, wasn't about being the strongest or the fastest or the fittest. It was about sticking with it and not giving up. It meant handling the mental stress of the workouts, which often included being yelled at and put down. "I can definitely do this!" Brandon said to himself.

First Phase lasts for six weeks. A lot of guys quit or became disqualified during this phase. Brandon's long months on air-craft carriers had made him soft for the kind of physical exercises he now had to do. His performance caught the attention of the extremely tough instructors right away. They identified him as a weak link. They called him out every time they saw the tiniest weakness in him. There is a saying in BUD/S training: "Don't be that guy." "That guy" is the one the instructors pick on and give the worst punishments to. To Brandon's dismay, he was "that guy."

Every day the training began at 5:00 A.M. on the beach, with grueling exercises. By the second week Brandon's hands were raw with open wounds from doing what felt like endless push-ups on the wet sand. He tried to ignore the poor state of his hands and just keep going. However, the condition of his hands made some exercises even more challenging. This included exercises that involved catching and swinging from ropes, climbing up and over walls, or holding on to or gripping things.

The BUD/S O-course, a killer obstacle course, even for anyone in the best condition, was packed with exactly those kinds of activities. SEAL recruits are expected to do the entire course in fifteen minutes or less. From start to finish, the O-course stations are:

Parallel bars.

Shimmy along a set of steel tubes slanted at an upward angle for 12 feet.

Tires.

Step through multiple tires as rapidly as possible.

Low wall.

Jump up and swing over an 8-foot plywood wall.

High wall.

Climb up and over a wall double the height of the low wall using a thick rope.

Low barbed-wire crawl.

Crawl under barbed wire, staying as low to the ground as possible.

100-foot-high cargo net.

Climb up and over.

Balance logs.

Stay balanced while running over a series of rolling logs.

Hooyah logs.

Holding hands above the head, step up and over a pile of 3-foot logs.

Rope transfer.

Climb up one rope, transfer to another, then slide down.

Dirty Name.

Jump up and grab the first of two log beams. Pull up onto the beam, and with

The cargo net is part of the SEAL obstacle course, or O-course, which is run on a weekly basis during SEAL training.

feet planted, jump onto the second, higher log beam. Then swing around and over, and drop down to the sand. This station is so named because a false move can lead to broken ribs.

Weaver.

Weave over and under, way up, then down and out of a series of metal bars spaced about 3 feet apart and shaped like a shallow triangle.

Burma Bridge.

Climb a 15-foot rope, then transition to an unstable rope bridge, cross the bridge, and slide down a second 15-foot rope on the other side.

Hooyah logs again.

Slide for Life.

Climb to the top of a four-story set of platforms with an angled rope that slopes down about 100 feet to the bottom. Then mount the rope from the bottom with legs wrapped around, hang using arms, and inchworm down the rope. Next, transition to an assault style on top position (much quicker). Those who fall off have a good chance of being severely injured and medically disqualified from BUD/S.

A soldier crosses the Burma Bridge during the weekly O-course.

Rope swing.

Grab the rope while running and swing up. Then let go at just the right moment to hop up and onto a high balance log beam.

Tires again.

Incline wall.

Scoot up, then slide over and down the wall.

Spider wall.

Climb up and shimmy sideways along a high plywood-and-log wall in a way that is similar to rock climbing, using finger and toe strength.

Vaults.

Jump up and over each in a series of logs set up at intervals. Then sprint to the finish.

When it was Brandon's turn, he didn't think about his hands or about being "that guy." He only thought about the course ahead. He got off to a great start, but by the time he got to the Weaver he started to slow down. He was getting winded. By the time he reached the Slide for Life, he felt completely out of gas.

Brandon found himself hanging on to the ropes of the Slide for Life for dear life. He couldn't ignore his hands any longer. His grip strength was gone, and now he was four stories up and upside down. He hooked his elbows over the top of the ropes to try to give his hands a minute to recover.

One of the instructors, Kowalski, saw this immediately. "Webb," he shouted, "you have two seconds to let go of that rope with your elbows. Those two seconds are up!" He ordered Brandon to shimmy down the regular way, by using his hands with his legs.

Brandon tried to do what he was instructed to. He unhooked his elbows but could not grip the rope with his hands. He dangled upside down by his legs. He had no choice. He let go.

Within seconds, Brandon fell four stories and hit the hard ground. He could not believe he had fallen off the Slide for Life. He also could not believe that he wasn't badly hurt.

Instructor Kowalski walked over. "Are you all right?" he asked without any real concern.

"Hooyah, Instructor Kowalski," Brandon managed to get out.

"Well, then get up and get going!" Kowalski yelled.

That is exactly what Brandon did. After that the instructors were even more rough on him. But Brandon refused to break. Instead it fueled his desire to succeed. Over the next few weeks the instructors saw that no matter what they dished out, Brandon was handling it. This guy was not going to quit. Soon he went from being "that guy" to being the "gray man." The "gray man" is someone no one notices because he is the guy who does everything just right and doesn't stand out.

Brandon and only 70 of his original

220 classmates made it through to Second Phase. Second Phase focuses on water skills. Even though Brandon had all that experience from his years on the *Peace* and from being in the Navy for a few years, he still had a lot to learn.

Teamwork is essential when hauling 600-pound logs during physical training exercises.

One of the most important things he learned was not to make any assumptions when going into a challenge. "No matter what I know, or *think* I know," he realized, "I have to keep my ego in check and see what I can learn."

Third Phase started with just 50 members from Class 215. Third Phase is nine weeks of SEAL-style land warfare. It includes basic soldiering skills, explosives and demolition, marksmanship, land navigation, and reconnaissance. And lots more physical conditioning.

By the time Third Phase ended, there were just twenty men left. About ninety percent of the class had washed out. There were a few more months of training ahead before Brandon and the others would officially become Navy SEALs. But it was also time to pick which team he'd like to be assigned to. Brandon's top choice was Team 3. He picked Team 3 because its area of operations was in the Middle East. Even though there was no major fighting going on in any part of the world, Brandon figured that the Middle East was a hot spot for future conflicts. SEAL Team 3 also had a good reputation. Brandon was delighted when he heard that he had been assigned to Team 3.

In late 1998 Brandon passed his boards, the last hurdle to officially becoming a Navy SEAL. When the Navy SEAL Trident badge was pinned to his uniform, it was one of the proudest moments of Brandon's life.

Two boat crews during the Second Phase of SEAL training.

A sniper takes aim aboard a Seahawk helicopter during aerial sniper training.

CHAPTER

7

What did Brandon do after he became a Navy SEAL? He went for more training. "SEALs never stop training," he said. "When we aren't actually deployed, we're always learning new skills. We continue to practice our existing skills. And we have to keep ourselves in top physical condition."

One day, Brandon and his buddy Glen were called in to see their officer in charge, Lieutenant McNary. They had no idea what this was about. Without saying a word, they looked at each other nervously. "Are we in some sort of trouble?" Brandon wondered.

The exact opposite turned out to be the case. "You guys have done a really good job here," said McNary. "And we're shorthanded on snipers right now. We want to offer you both the opportunity to go to sniper school."

Brandon and Glen looked at each other. This wasn't something Brandon had ever considered. For one thing, it was unheard of for new guys to get into sniper school, let alone be *asked* to go. For another thing, as hard as BUD/S is, SEAL sniper school is even harder. It is three months of twelve-plus-hour days, seven days a week. It is considered one of the toughest programs anywhere. It is so tough that no one is looked down on for failing to complete it. They are respected just for getting in.

It was an opportunity neither Brandon nor Glen could pass up. They entered sniper school in the spring of 2000. There were twenty-four other guys. Only half the class would graduate.

There are two main parts to sniper school. The first part is the shooting phase. The second part is the stalking phase.

The shooting phase is all about

weapons. Brandon learned everything about guns and bullets, inside and out. In the shooting phase, Brandon learned to be a precision marksman. He and Glen were paired together to take turns as the shooter and the spotter. The shooter's job is to concentrate on making a perfect shot. He uses information the spotter gives him to do that. The spotter tells the shooter about the wind. He watches how the bullets travel through the air, and tells the shooter. And much more.

Brandon and Glen were a good team. Glen was a naturally gifted marksman. Brandon seemed to have a natural gift for reading the wind. He could figure out all the surrounding conditions. This may have had something to do with his knowing how to "read" water currents and the stars.

The stalking phase started with classes on stealth and movement. Brandon learned how to use vegetation to camouflage himself and his weapon. He learned about how to use and hide behind things for cover. He practiced building hide sites in the earth. A hide site provides cover and, in the desert—where Brandon was

Two team members work together to take out standing pop-up targets.

headed with SEAL Team 3—it would also provide some relief from the intense heat.

Stalking drills were incredibly difficult. Brandon and the others had to inch up on a target and take a shot. They had to do this without being seen by the instructors. Two instructors with high-powered binoculars were positioned in a command tower. From there they could see the entire area. They were in communication by radio with three or more walkers on the ground. If an instructor saw a sniper student move, he told a walker. The walker went over to the moving stalker and said, "You're busted. You've failed the stalk."

Brandon failed his first stalk. An instructor didn't see him. He simply ran out of time. He was determined that that was not going to happen again. And it didn't. In fact, he became so good at the stalking phase that he helped several of his classmates practice before the final test.

Brandon and Glen both passed. Brandon was now a Navy SEAL sniper. He graduated on June 12, 2000. It was his twenty-sixth birthday. It was almost ten years to the day his father had thrown him off the boat.

A SEAL fires a sniper rifle during a training flight.

Two soldiers prepare charges to blow up material left by al Qaeda troops.

CHAPTER

8

Shortly after graduation, Brandon was deployed to the Middle East. He served aboard the USS *Duluth* on a mission to stop Iraqi oil smugglers.

Immediately after September 11, 2001, when he deployed overseas again, Brandon was sent to Kuwait. His mission was similar. His platoon helped stop oil smugglers.

Both al Qaeda and the Taliban had large operations in Afghanistan. Brandon really wanted to be there. He wanted to directly help stop terrorists. But he knew this work in Kuwait was important. The SEALs had been supporting this

The ECHO platoon gathered at Kandahar International Airport.

effort since 1990. And his team did stop a terrorist boat while in Kuwait.

Then, on October 7, 2001, President George W. Bush announced Operation Enduring Freedom. The United States and the United Kingdom were going to join forces. They were going to work with the Afghan United Front. The goal was to destroy al Qaeda and Taliban training camps in Afghanistan. Brandon's platoon was sent there to join the action.

In early December, Brandon's platoon arrived in Afghanistan. Kandahar International Airport was now a base of operations for armed forces fighting the terrorists. There were Special Operations teams from eight different countries fighting together. The countries were

Australia, Canada, Denmark, Germany, New Zealand, Norway, Turkey, and the United States.

On Christmas Day, Brandon's platoon went on their first patrol in Afghanistan. Brandon noticed that the environment was different from Kuwait. Kuwait was a sandy desert. Afghanistan had much rougher terrain. The patrol was a good introduction to the area.

A few days later, members of Brandon's platoon went to a place called Tarnak Farms. It is where the 9/11 attackers are said to have trained. The SEALs went there to do some training themselves. They needed to test their weapons.

They arrived in two Humvees and got out. Brandon glanced down. He saw something sticking out from under one of the Humvees' tires. It looked like a pig's tail. He bent down to get a closer look. And froze.

"Hey, Brad," he called to one of the men. "Come take a look." Brad was an Explosive Ordnance Disposal (EOD) guy. This meant he was an expert at identifying explosives—and dismantling them. There were all kinds of land mines and

Brandon and a fellow SEAL at Afghan training camp Tarnak Farms.

handmade explosives in the ground all over Afghanistan. Brad and another EOD guy, Steve, took a close look at the scene.

"Okay, guys," Brad said. "We have parked directly on top of a mine."

Now everyone froze. They were stunned. How could their Humvee have parked on a mine without setting it off?

Brad and Steve carefully dismantled the mine. They found out that the mine had not been set up correctly. A terrorist's error had spared them all.

A Humvee exits a
landing craft.

ECHO PLATOON

CHAPTER

9

January 6, 2002, late afternoon
Zhawar Kili Caves
Khost, Afghanistan

It took Brandon's platoon about four hours to clear all the caves. The work was tiresome and nerve-racking at the same time.

They went back into the caves a second time. They gathered up documents and other things to take back. They planted explosives to blow up the caves later. They recorded the exact entrances to each cave. This was for the next air strikes. The air strikes would be more accurate with this information. Some of the men documented everything with videos and photos.

Then, before they left, they blew up the ammunition they had found. The explosion created a huge fireball on the mountain. "It may be January," thought Brandon, "but it sure looks like the Fourth of July."

Daylight was starting to fade. The men made the long trek back to where the helicopters would pick them up.

Brandon and the others waited. They had had a long day. They had done a

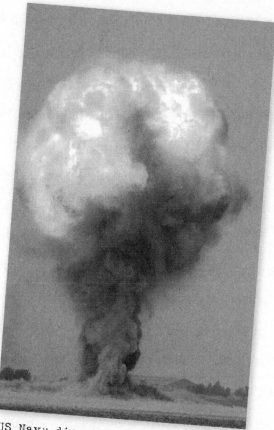

US Navy disposal technicians destroy tanks, rifles, and ammunition seized during support missions.

good job. They were ready to leave and get some rest.

One of the EOD techs, Steve, started to dump out his water. He had a lot of water bottles with him. The water was for making blasting charges. The water was heavy to carry. Since their work was done, Steve didn't think he needed the water anymore.

"Hey dude," said Brandon. "Give me the rest. I'll take it." Steve gladly handed Brandon the bottles he had left.

Soon the men heard the sound of the helicopters. The choppers sounded like they were about five to ten minutes away. Then, to everyone's surprise, the sound of the choppers started to fade. They were heading *away* from the men. Why?

The captain at the command center was impressed with how much the men had found. He wanted them to stay longer. He wanted them to search the entire area near the caves. So he called the choppers back. The men would be staying.

Brandon had just polished off the last of Steve's water. Steve suddenly wished he had kept it. There was no extra water. The men did not have proper clothing. It got very cool at night in the mountains. They did not have supplies to set up a real camp.

And they were in enemy territory.

The men found an abandoned village not far from the caves. Four men went with their chief to clear it. It was completely deserted. The village became the platoon's new base of operations for the rest of the mission.

A soldier inspects a satellite-guided bomb.

CHAPTER

10

January 7, 2002
Zhawar Kili Caves
Khost, Afghanistan

The next morning the men got back to work. They split up to gather more information. Brandon went out with three other guys—Brad, Cassidy, and Osman—before dawn. There had been fighting the night before. Terrorists on the ground had exchanged fire with a heavily armed

US C-130 gunship flying overhead. The men were headed to the battle site nearby. The site was in the same mountain range where Brandon and his platoon currently were. It was their job to look for bodies.

They reached the site just before day-break. Almost immediately, they heard voices. The voices were coming from the caves above them. There were bodies there, all right—live ones!

Brandon, Cassidy, Osman, and Brad hit the ground. Their eyes were glued on the caves. Suddenly, enemy fighters started to pour out of one of the caves. There were at least twenty of them. They were all armed.

Brandon and the others were outnum-bered. Plus, they were not armed for battle.

The terrorists were headed their way. They had not seen Brandon and the others. Yet.

There was only one thing the SEALs could do. They needed to call in an air strike. Fast.

Luckily, there was a B-52 bomber jet nearby. As quietly as he could, Brad got them on the radio. Now it was Brandon's

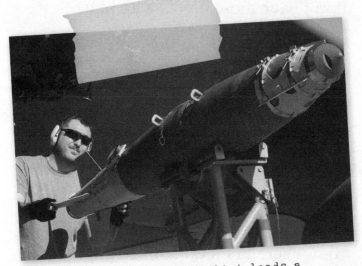

An armament systems specialist loads a 500-pound Joint Direct Attack Munition, or JDAM.

job to give the guys in the jet the terrorists' exact location. The bombers can be very accurate. They are like snipers in the sky.

Brandon had radioed locations to bomber jets before. However, when he did that in the past, he used special equipment. He used a high-powered laser range finder and a GPS. Today, he didn't have those things with him.

Brandon had to rely on his training. He had to use all his senses and his gut instinct, too. The B-52 would be dropping 1,000-pound JDAMs from 20,000 feet up in the air. The bombs would fall close to the speed of sound.

The terrorists were less than 500 yards from where Brandon and his guys were.

If he called in the wrong numbers, the bombs would miss the terrorists. The bombs might hit him and the others instead.

Brandon quickly tried to figure out the correct distance. He thought back to sniper school. There, they were told to visualize something familiar. Like a football field. Then you figure out if your distance is one football field. Or two. Or three and a half. Or whatever. That kind of estimating worked best with level ground. Brandon and the guys were not on level ground. They were on a rugged, rocky mountain.

The morning light also didn't help. It made it harder for Brandon to be sure about the distance.

Brandon's mind scrambled to work out the numbers. In the meantime, the terrorists kept heading toward him and the others. "Brandon!" Cassidy whispered. "You need to do this now!"

Brandon gave Cassidy numbers to

Lt. Cassidy scans the desert for danger.

radio up to the B-52. He figured out a location that he thought would be about 100 meters past the terrorists. This was in the opposite direction of himself and his guys. He reasoned that if he was right, the bombs would drop behind the terrorists. That would buy him a few seconds to adjust his numbers. Then he would call in a more accurate location for a second strike.

The SEALs needed to head for cover. They needed to be behind something when the terrorists finally spotted them. They needed to protect themselves from incoming fire.

When the SEALs ran for cover, the terrorists saw them. They shouted to one another in alarm. Then they started to shoot.

From their cover, Brandon heard the distinct *crack!* of gunfire. They were followed by the *snap!* of bullets breaking the sound barrier.

Brandon and his guys returned fire. Brandon glanced up for a brief second. The B-52 was so high he couldn't see or hear it. But he saw vapor trails in the sky. He knew the first bombs were about to drop.

Brad got the call that the bombs were on the way. They would hit within seconds. The SEALs dropped to the ground and rolled in the opposite direction. They opened their mouths to protect their lungs. An impact this size, this close, would rock their chests. If they kept their mouths closed, their lungs might burst.

The first set of JDAMs shook the mountain. Rubble scattered everywhere. Brandon whipped around to see where the bombs had hit. "Yes!" he said. "They hit about one hundred yards behind the terrorists."

He quickly adjusted the numbers in his head. He shouted them to Cassidy. Cassidy gave them to Brad. Brad gave them to the guys in the B-52. Then they waited.

Brandon focused on his breathing. He made it slow and steady. He breathed in the cool morning air. The air was mixed with the smell of explosives. He knew his numbers were accurate this time.

Within minutes the second strike was on its way. The guys opened their mouths, ducked, and rolled.

The second drop took out all the terrorists.

Every day of war is serious business. Battles large and small are fought. Lives are lost so other lives can be saved.

Brandon, Cassidy, Osman, and Brad went back to their temporary base. They would be there another week.

Supplies were flown in for the platoon. There was a lot of enemy activity in the area. The men went out on patrol to collect information. They also found a lot of weapons. They captured a few prisoners, too.

One day, they were clearing another village. They did not find any people. They did find a lot of plans, notes, and weapons. Suddenly, something moved. What was it?

The men watched as a small, light tan puppy trotted toward them. This was the last thing anyone expected to see! "Hey, little fellow," said Brandon. He and the others surrounded the puppy, who was very playful. The men named the puppy J-Dam. He became the platoon's mascot.

J-Dam was rescued by US Navy Special Forces.

SEALs talk with Afghan locals during an expedition.

CHAPTER 11

January 11, 2002
Village near the Zhawar Kili Caves
Khost, Afghanistan

The platoon went into another village. They had been watching this village for a few days. The people there looked like farmers. But the soldiers were not one hundred percent sure they really were. They thought that at least some of them could be terrorists. The SEALs went to get a closer look at the place and the people.

Brandon set up in sniper position. He hid in a spot that let him see the village. He watched everything. He guarded his platoon. He was ready to protect them if they needed him.

He looked through the scope on his .300 Win Mag sniper rifle. It showed him everything up close. He saw Cassidy and the team enter the village. He saw some

SEALs search for al Qaeda and Taliban among Afghan mountain villages.

of the villagers suddenly rush around.

"Why are they doing that?" Brandon wondered. It seemed suspicious to him. But he wasn't sure. He radioed Cassidy. "Be on your toes," he said. "There may be something going on."

Brandon looked back and forth between his team and the farmers. Then he saw one man standing off to the side. He had a rifle. It was slung casually over the man's shoulder. The man seemed totally relaxed. Brandon thought he was just a farmer. But why was he carrying a gun? Alarm bells started to go off in Brandon's head.

The man with the rifle was about 600 yards away from Brandon. That was a distance of about six football fields.

Brandon knew he could take out the man with one shot. No problem.

Brandon kept his finger on his rifle's trigger. "If this guy is innocent," he reasoned, "shooting him would be a big mistake." He knew it could also create a dangerous scene. On the other hand, his team could be in danger if the man *wasn't* innocent.

Brandon knew he had all the information he was going to get. "Do I take the shot or not?" he asked himself.

It all came down to his instincts. He watched the man with the rifle. Something still did not feel right. But he decided not to take the shot.

Brandon watched as Cassidy and the team went up to the farmers. He watched the two groups talking. Suddenly, he saw something off to his left. It was someone in Arab dress. This guy was clearly not an Afghan farmer. And he was hightailing it out of there. Brandon watched the guy scramble up a little goat trail into the mountains.

This must be what Brandon had been sensing. The farmers were hiding this guy. It explained why that farmer had a rifle. Who was the guy running away? Was he a member of al Qaeda? Brandon

Seeing through a sniper's eyes.

did not know. All he knew was that the farmers had hidden him. Now they had helped him get away.

Brandon switched to his binoculars. He watched the guy scurry up the path. Brandon knew he could not get an accurate shot off before the guy disappeared. He radioed Cassidy and told him what had happened. Then he watched Cassidy and the farmers argue.

Later, Brandon thought back over everything. He did not regret his decision. The others agreed with him. They all knew that mountain villagers sometimes hid terrorists. For the most part, though, the local people were good people. They were just trying to get along and survive. They wanted to keep living in the mountains. It was where their families had lived for generations.

Brandon's platoon was supposed to spend just twelve hours on that mountain in Khost. They wound up being there for nine days. They explored more than seventy caves and tunnels. They found nearly one million pounds of ammunition and equipment. They uncovered plans and other information about the enemy. They also captured many prisoners.

The US military dropped more than 400,000 pounds of bombs on the area. The SEALs had completed their mission. They had shut down one of the biggest terrorist training camps in Afghanistan.

Brandon Webb and two "friendlies"—Afghan allies.

A FEW WORDS FROM BRANDON WEBB

few months after our mission at the caves, my platoon left Afghanistan.

The following year, I was asked to help rewrite the course of study for the SEAL sniper school. I did this with my fellow SEAL and friend Eric Davis. It was a tremendous honor and responsibility.

In mid-2006 I made the decision to leave the Navy. I wanted to spend more time with my family. I also started a new career. I now run a media company about Special Ops.

Being a Navy SEAL sniper is important and incredibly serious work. Having a job where you may have to take another life should always be exactly that. Nothing should be taken lightly. Your own life may depend upon it.

Got that? Well, here are a few other things I hope you take away from reading this book. I think I was a pretty average kid. What set me apart? I had a desire to succeed at whatever I did. I also had a strong dream to become a Navy SEAL.

Don't have a dream of your own yet

about what you want to be when you grow up? Don't worry. You will some-day. There will be something that you are really crazy about. Figure out how to turn that passion into a career. Stay focused. Be determined. Bring excellence to whatever you do. And be sure to approach your life's mission like a Navy SEAL: Never quit.